GUT FEELINGS

How Your Diet Shapes Your Mental Health

M.A. Cordova

CONTENTS

Title Page

Chapter 1: The Magic of the Gut-Brain Connection   1

How Your Gut Influences Your Mood   3

The Role of Microbiota in Mental Health   5

Chapter 2: Food as Fuel for Your Mind   7

The Science Behind Comfort Foods   9

Eating for Energy and Focus   11

Chapter 3: Diet and Its Impact on Anxiety   13

The Link Between Sugar and Stress   16

The Role of Omega-3 Fatty Acids   18

Chapter 4: Battling Depression with Nutrition   20

The Importance of a Balanced Diet   22

Success Stories: Diet Changes That Helped   24

Chapter 5: The Power of Probiotics   26

Fermented Foods for a Happier Gut   28

How Probiotics Can Improve Mental Clarity   30

Chapter 6: Mindful Eating for Mental Wellness   32

Listening to Your Body's Signals   34

Creating a Positive Eating Environment   36

Chapter 7: Meal Planning for a Healthy Mind   38

How to Create a Mood-Boosting Grocery List   40

Quick and Nutritious Recipes to Try   42

Chapter 8: Overcoming Food Myths   44

The Truth About Fad Diets and Mental Health   46

Embracing a Sustainable Eating Habit   48

Chapter 9: The Role of Lifestyle in Mental Health   50

Sleep: Resting for a Sharper Mind   52

Stress Management Techniques   54

Chapter 10: Your Journey to a Healthier Mind and Gut   56

Building a Support System   58

Celebrating Small Wins on Your Path to Wellness   60

CHAPTER 1: THE MAGIC OF THE GUT-BRAIN CONNECTION

Understanding the Gut-Brain Axis

The gut-brain axis is an incredible and complex communication network that links your digestive system with your brain. Imagine a two-way highway where messages are constantly traveling back and forth, influencing everything from your mood to your mental clarity. This connection is vital for understanding how what you eat can drastically affect your mental health. The gut is often referred to as the "second brain" because it produces a significant amount of neurotransmitters, including serotonin, which plays a crucial role in regulating mood and anxiety levels. Recognizing this connection can empower you to make dietary choices that support not only your physical health but also your emotional well-being.

Your diet is the primary fuel for your gut microbiome, a vibrant community of trillions of microorganisms that live in your intestines. These little powerhouses help digest your food, synthesize vitamins, and even produce short-chain fatty acids that have been linked to reduced inflammation and improved mood. When you nourish your gut with a diverse array of fruits, vegetables, whole grains, and healthy fats, you're not just feeding your body; you're also nurturing your mind. On the flip side, a diet high in processed foods, sugars, and unhealthy fats can disrupt this delicate balance, leading to gut dysbiosis, which is often associated with anxiety and depression.

Research shows that a healthy gut can enhance your brain function and emotional resilience. For example, studies have revealed that probiotics, which are beneficial bacteria found in fermented foods like yogurt and kimchi, can boost your mood and reduce symptoms of depression. This is because they help maintain the integrity of the gut barrier, preventing harmful substances from entering the bloodstream and triggering inflammation. Incorporating these foods into your diet can be a delicious way to support your mental health, transforming your meals into powerful tools for emotional stability.

Moreover, the gut-brain axis also highlights the importance of mindful eating. Paying attention to how different foods affect your mood and energy levels can lead to healthier choices. Have you ever noticed that after a sugary snack, you experience a quick energy boost followed by a crash? This rollercoaster can contribute to anxiety and irritability. By being aware of these patterns, you can make smarter dietary choices that keep your energy steady and your mood balanced. Focus on whole, nutrient-dense foods that not only taste great but also support your mental clarity and emotional well-being.

In conclusion, understanding the gut-brain axis is a game-changer in the conversation about food and mental health. By recognizing the profound impact your diet has on your mood, anxiety levels, and overall mental clarity, you can take actionable steps towards a healthier lifestyle. Embrace foods that nourish both your gut and your mind, and watch as your emotional well-being flourishes. Every meal is an opportunity to support your mental health—let's make those choices count!

THE ROLE OF MICROBIOTA IN MENTAL HEALTH

The relationship between our gut microbiota and mental health is a captivating area of research that reveals just how interconnected our bodies really are. Imagine a bustling city within your gut, filled with trillions of microorganisms working tirelessly to keep your body functioning smoothly. These tiny residents, known as microbiota, play a crucial role not only in digestion but also in regulating mood, emotions, and overall mental health. It's a remarkable discovery that the foods we consume can influence this intricate ecosystem and, in turn, our mental well-being.

Emerging studies suggest that a diverse microbiota can promote resilience against mental health challenges like anxiety and depression. When we nourish our gut with a variety of foods —especially fiber-rich fruits, vegetables, and fermented items— we encourage a thriving community of beneficial bacteria. These friendly microbes produce neurotransmitters, such as serotonin, which is often called the "feel-good" hormone. In fact, a staggering 90% of serotonin is produced in the gut! By prioritizing a gut-friendly diet, we can support these microbial allies in their mission to boost our mood and enhance our mental clarity.

On the flip side, diets high in processed foods, sugar, and unhealthy fats can disrupt this delicate balance, leading to an overgrowth of harmful bacteria. This imbalance can trigger inflammation, which has been linked to a host of mental health issues. When our gut microbiota is out of whack, it can lead to feelings of anxiety, irritability, and even depression. Understanding this connection empowers us to make healthier choices that can positively impact our mental state. It's a powerful reminder that what we eat truly matters—not just for our physical health, but for our emotional well-being as well.

Integrating gut-friendly foods into your daily routine can be both fun and delicious. Experimenting with new recipes that include probiotics, like yogurt, kefir, and sauerkraut, can add a tasty twist to your meals. Additionally, incorporating prebiotic foods like garlic, onions, and bananas can help feed those beneficial bacteria. This journey towards better mental health through diet can be an exciting adventure. Sharing recipes and meal ideas with friends can turn healthy eating into a social activity, making it easier to stick to these positive changes.

As you explore the fascinating world of gut microbiota and its influence on mental health, remember that small actions can lead to significant changes. By making mindful food choices, you can cultivate a healthier gut and, in turn, a happier mind. Embrace the power of your diet and take charge of your mental well-being. The journey may require some effort, but the rewards—a brighter mood, increased energy, and improved mental clarity—are absolutely worth it!

CHAPTER 2: FOOD AS FUEL FOR YOUR MIND

Nutrients That Boost Brain Power

The food you choose to fuel your body can have a profound impact on your brain health. Young adults and teens are at a pivotal stage in their lives, where academic pressures, social dynamics, and mental health challenges converge. Understanding how to harness the power of nutrients to boost brain function can be a game changer. The right diet can enhance memory, improve focus, and even stabilize mood, making it essential to pay attention to what you eat.

Omega-3 fatty acids are a standout nutrient that deserves the spotlight. Found abundantly in fatty fish like salmon, walnuts, and flaxseeds, these essential fats are crucial for maintaining brain cell structure and function. Research has shown that omega-3s can help reduce symptoms of anxiety and depression, making them a must-add to your weekly meal plan. Incorporating these brain-boosting foods into your diet not only promotes optimal cognitive function but also supports your overall emotional well-being.

Antioxidants, such as vitamins C and E, play a significant role in protecting the brain from oxidative stress. Berries, dark chocolate, and leafy greens are packed with these powerhouse nutrients. They help combat inflammation and can improve communication between brain cells, which is vital for effective cognitive processing. By indulging in a colorful array of fruits and vegetables, you're not just treating your taste buds; you're also arming your brain with the tools it needs to thrive in a demanding world.

Another nutrient that should not be overlooked is B vitamins, particularly B6, B12, and folate. These vitamins are essential for the production of neurotransmitters, the brain's chemical messengers, which regulate mood and cognitive function. Foods like eggs, legumes, and leafy greens can help you maintain optimal levels of these essential vitamins. A well-rounded intake of B vitamins can enhance energy levels, boost concentration, and keep anxiety at bay, allowing you to tackle your daily challenges with confidence.

Lastly, don't underestimate the power of hydration. Water plays a crucial role in overall brain function and mental clarity. Dehydration can lead to fatigue, reduced attention span, and even mood swings. Make it a habit to drink water throughout the day, and consider incorporating hydrating foods like cucumbers, oranges, and melons into your meals. By prioritizing hydration alongside nutrient-rich foods, you'll cultivate an environment where your brain can flourish, leading to improved mental health and resilience. Embrace these dietary changes, and you'll not only feel better but also think better!

THE SCIENCE BEHIND COMFORT FOODS

Comfort foods have a special place in our hearts and our kitchens, often evoking feelings of nostalgia and warmth. But what exactly is happening in our bodies and brains when we indulge in these beloved dishes? The science behind comfort foods reveals a fascinating interplay between the psychological and physiological effects of what we eat. When we consume foods that we associate with comfort—like creamy mac and cheese or warm chocolate chip cookies—our brains release a cocktail of chemicals that can significantly influence our mood and emotional state.

One of the key players in this process is serotonin, a neurotransmitter often referred to as the "feel-good" hormone. Many comfort foods are rich in carbohydrates, which can increase the availability of tryptophan, an amino acid that the body converts into serotonin. This boost in serotonin levels can lead to feelings of happiness and relaxation, making those cozy meals not just delicious but also a powerful tool for mental well-being. It's no wonder that a bowl of pasta or a slice of cake can feel like a warm hug on a tough day!

Moreover, the gut-brain connection plays a pivotal role in how comfort foods impact our mental health. The gut is often referred to as the "second brain" because it houses a complex network of neurons and is home to trillions of microorganisms that influence our mood and behavior. When we enjoy our favorite comfort foods, we're not just treating our taste buds; we're nurturing our gut microbiome. A healthy gut flora can enhance the production of neurotransmitters, further supporting our mental health. So, that pizza night with friends might be doing more for your happiness than you realize!

The emotional aspect of comfort foods should not be overlooked either. Many of these foods are tied to cherished memories or cultural traditions. Eating them can trigger a sense of belonging and security, which is crucial for young adults and teens navigating the ups and downs of life. Sharing a meal with loved ones while enjoying comforting flavors can foster connections and create a supportive environment, reinforcing the idea that food can be a source of joy and community, not just sustenance.

In conclusion, the science behind comfort foods extends far beyond mere indulgence. Understanding how these foods influence our brain chemistry and gut health reveals their potential to help us manage anxiety and depression. So, the next time you reach for your favorite comfort dish, remember that it's not just about the immediate pleasure; it's about nourishing your mind and soul. Embracing the joy of comfort foods can be a delicious and fulfilling way to support your mental health journey.

EATING FOR ENERGY AND FOCUS

Eating for energy and focus is not just about fueling your body; it's about supercharging your mind! Imagine waking up each day feeling vibrant, alert, and ready to conquer whatever comes your way. The key lies in understanding how the foods you choose can significantly impact your mental clarity and emotional well-being. By making smart food choices, you can boost your brainpower and enhance your focus, making it easier to tackle school, work, or any challenges that come your way.

First, let's talk about the incredible benefits of nutrient-dense foods. Whole grains, fruits, vegetables, lean proteins, and healthy fats are not just good for your waistline; they are essential for brain health! Whole grains provide a steady source of energy, preventing those dreaded sugar crashes that leave you feeling sluggish and unfocused. Incorporating colorful fruits and veggies into your meals not only adds vibrancy to your plate but also packs a punch of antioxidants, vitamins, and minerals that support cognitive function and overall mood. So, the next time you're reaching for a snack, think of the power that comes from nature's candy!

Healthy fats, like those found in avocados, nuts, and olive oil, play a significant role in brain function. Omega-3 fatty acids, in particular, are vital for maintaining optimal brain health. They help reduce inflammation and support the production of neurotransmitters, which are crucial for mood regulation. By including these healthy fats in your diet, you're not just satisfying your taste buds; you're also giving your brain the nutrients it needs to thrive. Plus, they can help combat feelings of anxiety and depression, making you feel more balanced and energized.

Don't forget the importance of hydration! Staying well-hydrated is essential for maintaining focus and concentration. Dehydration can lead to fatigue, irritability, and cognitive decline, making it harder to perform at your best. So, make it a habit to drink plenty of water throughout the day. If plain water feels a bit boring, spice it up with slices of lemon, cucumber, or fresh herbs. Staying hydrated will keep your mind sharp and your spirits lifted, allowing you to stay on top of your game.

Lastly, be mindful of how you structure your meals and snacks. Eating smaller, balanced meals throughout the day can help maintain steady energy levels, preventing the highs and lows associated with larger meals. Incorporate protein and fiber into your snacks to keep you feeling satisfied and focused. Think of snacks like Greek yogurt with berries, a handful of nuts, or whole-grain toast with avocado. These choices not only keep your energy levels stable but also contribute to a more positive mood. By embracing these delicious and nutritious foods, you'll be well on your way to achieving the energy and focus you need to thrive!

CHAPTER 3: DIET AND ITS IMPACT ON ANXIETY

Foods That Calm Your Nerves

In our fast-paced world, finding ways to soothe our minds is essential for maintaining balance and happiness. The foods we choose to consume can significantly impact our mental well-being, especially for young adults and teens navigating the complexities of life. Certain foods have the remarkable ability to calm your nerves and support emotional health, making them valuable allies in your quest for peace of mind. Let's explore some delightful options that can brighten your mood and strengthen the gut-brain connection!

First on the list are omega-3 fatty acids, predominantly found in fatty fish like salmon, mackerel, and sardines. These nutrient powerhouses are not only delicious but have also been linked to reduced symptoms of anxiety and depression. Omega-3s help in the production of neurotransmitters, like serotonin, which play a vital role in regulating mood. Incorporating these fish into your diet a couple of times a week can offer a tasty way to boost your mental health while enjoying a scrumptious meal. If you're not a fan of seafood, consider plant-based sources like flaxseeds and walnuts; they also pack a punch of omega-3 goodness!

Next, let's talk about colorful fruits and vegetables, bursting with vitamins, minerals, and antioxidants. Foods like berries, bananas, spinach, and sweet potatoes are fantastic for reducing oxidative stress in the body, a factor often linked to anxiety. Berries, in particular, are rich in antioxidants and vitamin C, which are known to help alleviate stress and boost your mood. The vibrant colors of fruits and veggies not only make your plate look appealing but also provide essential nutrients that support your gut health, leading to a happier mind. So, why not whip up a vibrant smoothie or a colorful salad to lift your spirits?

Fermented foods are another powerhouse category when it comes to calming your nerves. Items like yogurt, kefir, sauerkraut, and kimchi are packed with probiotics, the friendly bacteria that promote a healthy gut. A well-balanced gut microbiome is crucial for mental health, as it communicates with the brain through the gut-brain axis. Including fermented foods in your daily diet can enhance your mood and alleviate feelings of anxiety. Plus, they add a unique flavor and texture to your meals, making healthy eating an exciting adventure!

Lastly, let's not overlook the power of whole grains. Foods such as quinoa, brown rice, and oats are rich in fiber and essential nutrients that can help stabilize blood sugar levels. Fluctuating blood sugar can contribute to mood swings and irritability, making it essential to choose foods that provide sustained energy. Whole grains also promote the production of serotonin, the "feel-good" neurotransmitter, ensuring you remain calm and collected throughout your day. Start your morning with a hearty bowl of oatmeal topped with fruits and nuts, and feel the difference in your mood and energy levels!

Incorporating these foods into your diet is a delicious way to nurture your mental health while enjoying the tastes you love. By focusing on a balanced diet filled with omega-3s, vibrant fruits and veggies, fermented foods, and whole grains, you can create a strong foundation for emotional well-being. So, embrace these calming foods and embark on a nourishing journey that not only supports your gut health but also uplifts your spirit, helping you face life's challenges with confidence and joy!

THE LINK BETWEEN SUGAR AND STRESS

Sugar is often seen as a quick fix for a bad mood, but the relationship between sugar and stress is more complicated than it seems. Many young adults and teens turn to sugary snacks and drinks to boost their energy and improve their mood, especially during stressful times like exams or social pressures. However, this reliance on sugar can create a rollercoaster of highs and lows that ultimately contribute to increased anxiety and stress levels. The immediate satisfaction of a sugary treat is often followed by a crash, leaving you feeling even more depleted and anxious than before.

When we consume sugar, our bodies release a surge of insulin to help process it. This quick spike in blood sugar can result in a burst of energy, but it doesn't last long. As blood sugar levels drop, feelings of fatigue and irritability can set in, making stress feel even more overwhelming. For young women, who often juggle multiple responsibilities and societal expectations, this cycle can lead to chronic stress. It's crucial to recognize that while sugar may provide temporary relief, it can exacerbate feelings of anxiety and contribute to a tumultuous emotional state.

The gut-brain connection plays a key role in understanding how sugar impacts our mental health. When we consume sugar, it can alter the composition of the gut microbiome, which in turn influences our mood and stress levels. A healthy gut microbiome is essential for producing neurotransmitters like serotonin, often referred to as the "feel-good" hormone. However, a diet high in sugar can disrupt this balance, leading to an imbalance that may heighten feelings of anxiety and depression. For young adults and teens, maintaining a healthy gut can be a game-changer in managing stress and emotional well-being.

Moreover, the effects of sugar extend beyond just mood swings. Chronic sugar consumption has been linked to inflammation in the body, which can further exacerbate stress and anxiety. Inflammation has been shown to affect brain function and can lead to a variety of mental health issues. For those navigating the challenges of adolescence and early adulthood, understanding the physical consequences of a high-sugar diet is essential. Making small, intentional changes to reduce sugar intake can have profound effects on overall mental health and resilience.

In conclusion, the link between sugar and stress is a vital consideration for anyone looking to improve their mental well-being. Instead of reaching for that sugary snack during stressful moments, consider healthier alternatives that nourish both your body and mind. Whole foods, rich in nutrients and fiber, can stabilize blood sugar levels and support a healthy gut microbiome. By making informed dietary choices, young adults and teens can effectively manage stress and enhance their mental health, paving the way for a more balanced and fulfilling life.

THE ROLE OF OMEGA-3 FATTY ACIDS

The role of omega-3 fatty acids in our diets cannot be overstated, especially when it comes to mental health. These essential fats, primarily found in fish, flaxseeds, and walnuts, are like superheroes for our brains. They not only support cognitive function but also play a pivotal role in maintaining our mood. Research has shown that individuals who consume adequate amounts of omega-3s tend to report lower levels of anxiety and depression. Imagine the power of a simple dietary choice that could boost your mental state and help you feel more balanced!

One of the most exciting aspects of omega-3 fatty acids is their ability to influence the gut-brain connection. The gut and brain communicate through a complex network, and omega-3s help facilitate this dialogue. They promote the growth of beneficial gut bacteria, which in turn can produce neurotransmitters like serotonin, often referred to as the "feel-good" hormone. By nurturing your gut with omega-3-rich foods, you're not just feeding your body; you're also feeding your mind, creating a harmonious relationship between your gut health and mental well-being.

Incorporating omega-3s into your diet can be both delicious and enjoyable. Think about adding a serving of salmon to your weekly meal prep or snacking on a handful of walnuts. For those who prefer plant-based options, chia seeds and flaxseed meal can easily be sprinkled onto yogurt or blended into smoothies. The versatility of these foods means that you can find creative ways to include omega-3s in your meals, turning healthy eating into a fun and flavorful experience.

The impact of omega-3 fatty acids on mental health is backed by an increasing body of research. Studies suggest that higher levels of omega-3 intake are linked to a reduced risk of developing mood disorders. For young adults and teens navigating the ups and downs of life, understanding how nutrition influences these feelings can empower you to make choices that enhance your mental wellness. The effects of a balanced diet rich in omega-3s can be transformative, paving the way for clearer thinking and a more positive outlook.

As you embark on your journey to better mental health, remember that small changes can lead to significant benefits. Embracing omega-3 fatty acids is just one step toward nurturing your body and mind. By prioritizing these powerful nutrients, you're not only investing in your physical health but also taking charge of your emotional well-being. So, let's dive into the world of omega-3s and discover how they can elevate your mood and support your mental health like never before!

CHAPTER 4: BATTLING DEPRESSION WITH NUTRITION

Key Nutrients to Uplift Your Mood

The relationship between diet and mental health is gaining momentum, and for good reason! Certain nutrients play a pivotal role in shaping our mood and overall emotional well-being. Young adults and teens, who often face the pressures of life transitions, school, and social dynamics, can greatly benefit from understanding how food influences their feelings. By incorporating specific key nutrients into your diet, you can take positive steps toward managing anxiety and boosting your mood. Let's dive into some of these mood-lifting nutrients!

First up, we have omega-3 fatty acids. These powerful fats are not just essential for heart health; they're also crucial for brain function. Found in fatty fish like salmon, walnuts, and flaxseeds, omega-3s have been shown to reduce symptoms of depression and anxiety. They help to build brain cell membranes and promote communication between neurotransmitters, which are vital for a balanced mood. Making sure you get enough omega-3s can be a game-changer, especially during those overwhelming moments when stress levels spike.

Next on our nutrient list is vitamin D, often dubbed the "sunshine vitamin." Many young adults, especially those who spend a lot of time indoors, may find themselves lacking this essential vitamin.

Research indicates that low levels of vitamin D are linked to feelings of sadness and depression. The good news? You can boost your vitamin D levels through sunlight exposure, fortified foods, and supplements if necessary. Incorporating foods like fatty fish, egg yolks, and fortified dairy products into your meals can help you maintain optimal levels and keep your spirits high.

Don't forget about B vitamins, particularly B6, B12, and folate! These vitamins are essential for brain health and are involved in the production of neurotransmitters like serotonin and dopamine, which are crucial for mood regulation. Sources of B vitamins include leafy greens, whole grains, eggs, and legumes. By ensuring you have a good intake of these vitamins, you can help combat feelings of fatigue and irritability, paving the way for a happier, more energized you!

Lastly, let's shine a spotlight on magnesium. Often referred to as the "relaxation mineral," magnesium plays a significant role in managing stress and anxiety. It helps regulate neurotransmitters and can improve sleep quality, which is vital for mental health. Foods rich in magnesium include nuts, seeds, whole grains, and dark chocolate (yes, please!). By incorporating these foods into your diet, you'll be taking proactive steps to support your mind and body, helping you to feel more grounded and resilient.

Incorporating these key nutrients into your daily diet can create a noticeable shift in how you feel. Understanding the gut-brain connection and recognizing the impact of what you eat on your mental health empowers you to make informed choices. By embracing omega-3s, vitamin D, B vitamins, and magnesium, you are investing in your emotional well-being and setting the stage for a brighter, more vibrant future. So, let's get cooking and nourish our minds with the power of food!

THE IMPORTANCE OF A BALANCED DIET

A balanced diet is not just a trendy buzzword; it's a vital foundation for both physical and mental well-being. For young adults and teens navigating the complexities of life, food plays an essential role in shaping mood, energy levels, and overall mental health. The choices we make at meal times can significantly impact our gut health, which in turn affects our brain function. Imagine how invigorating it feels to know that what you eat can uplift your spirits, boost your confidence, and even enhance your cognitive abilities!

Incorporating a variety of nutrient-dense foods into your daily routine can create a powerhouse of positive effects. Fruits, vegetables, whole grains, and lean proteins work together to fuel your body while also nourishing your mind. These foods are packed with vitamins, minerals, and antioxidants that promote optimal brain function. Picture enjoying a colorful salad filled with leafy greens, vibrant peppers, and juicy berries. Not only does it look appealing, but it also provides the essential nutrients that support serotonin production, the "feel-good" hormone that can help alleviate feelings of anxiety and depression.

Additionally, the gut-brain connection is a fascinating area of research that reveals just how intertwined our digestive health is with our mental health. The gut is often referred to as the "second brain" because it produces neurotransmitters and communicates with the brain through various pathways. When we consume a balanced diet rich in fiber, healthy fats, and probiotics, we promote a thriving gut microbiome. This, in turn, can lead to improved mood regulation and cognitive function. Imagine feeling more focused and clear-headed simply by making smarter food choices!

However, it's essential to recognize that the journey to a balanced diet doesn't have to be complicated or restrictive. Instead of viewing it as a chore, embrace it as an exciting adventure! Experiment with new recipes, explore different cuisines, and savor the flavors of wholesome ingredients. Keep in mind that balance doesn't mean perfection; it's about making mindful choices that align with your lifestyle. Enjoying a slice of pizza or a scoop of ice cream occasionally is perfectly okay. The key is to ensure that the majority of your meals are nourishing and supportive of your mental wellness.

Ultimately, understanding the importance of a balanced diet empowers young adults and teens to take control of their health. By making conscious food choices, you can significantly impact your mental health and emotional resilience. Embrace the process of discovering what foods make you feel your best, and share that journey with friends and family. Not only will you feel better physically, but you will also cultivate a more positive mindset, ready to tackle life's challenges with confidence and enthusiasm!

SUCCESS STORIES: DIET CHANGES THAT HELPED

In the journey of understanding how our diets influence our mental health, numerous success stories shine a light on the transformative power of food choices. Young adults, teens, and women alike have discovered that simple changes in their eating habits can lead to remarkable improvements in their mood, energy levels, and overall mental well-being. These inspiring narratives not only motivate but also empower, showing that we all have the ability to take charge of our health through mindful dietary adjustments.

Take Sarah, for instance, a college student who struggled with anxiety and low energy. After researching the gut-brain connection, she decided to eliminate processed foods and incorporate more whole foods into her diet. By adding fermented foods like yogurt and kimchi, she noticed a significant shift in her mood and anxiety levels. Sarah's story exemplifies how embracing a nutrient-rich diet can foster a healthier mind, illustrating the direct impact of our food choices on our emotional state.

Then there's Mia, a high school senior who faced overwhelming stress and bouts of depression during exam season. Seeking relief, she turned to a plant-based diet, focusing on fruits, vegetables, and whole grains. Mia's commitment to eating foods rich in omega-3 fatty acids, like chia seeds and walnuts, not only enhanced her cognitive function but also elevated her spirits. Her experience highlights the importance of specific nutrients in combating mental health challenges, proving that what we eat can indeed be a game-changer.

Another powerful story is that of Jessica, a working professional who battled chronic fatigue and mood swings. After consulting with a nutritionist, she learned about the effects of sugar on mental health. By cutting back on sugary snacks and replacing them with healthy fats and protein-rich foods, Jessica found herself more focused and less irritable. Her journey underscores the importance of listening to our bodies and understanding how different foods can either uplift or drain our mental energy.

Finally, we cannot overlook the story of Emma, a young mother who experienced postpartum depression. Determined to find relief, she began to focus on her gut health by incorporating a variety of fiber-rich foods and probiotics into her diet. The changes she made not only helped her regain her mental clarity but also allowed her to connect more deeply with her baby. Emma's success reinforces the idea that diet is a crucial player in our emotional resilience and highlights how nourishing our bodies can lead to profound mental health benefits.

CHAPTER 5: THE POWER OF PROBIOTICS

What Are Probiotics and Why They Matter

Probiotics are live microorganisms that provide a plethora of health benefits when consumed in adequate amounts. Often referred to as "good" or "friendly" bacteria, these tiny allies predominantly reside in our gut, where they play a crucial role in maintaining a balanced microbiome. This balance is essential for not only digestive health but also for overall well-being. Imagine your gut as a bustling city, where probiotics act as the helpful neighbors ensuring that everything runs smoothly. When we consume foods rich in probiotics, such as yogurt, kefir, sauerkraut, and kimchi, we are essentially feeding our gut good vibes, setting the stage for a happier, healthier life.

Why do probiotics matter? The answer lies in their profound impact on our mental health. Research has increasingly highlighted the gut-brain connection, revealing that our gut health is closely linked to our emotions and mental state. The gut produces a significant amount of neurotransmitters, including serotonin, often dubbed the "feel-good hormone." When our gut flora is imbalanced, it can lead to decreased serotonin production, which may contribute to feelings of anxiety and depression. By incorporating probiotics into our diets, we can support a healthy gut microbiome, ultimately paving the way for improved mood and mental resilience.

Moreover, probiotics can enhance our immune system, which is essential for young adults and teens navigating the stresses of school, work, and social life. A strong immune system helps fend off illnesses that can take a toll on both physical and mental health. When we get sick, stress levels can rise, leading to a cycle that exacerbates anxiety and depressive symptoms. By prioritizing probiotics in our diets, we are not only nurturing our gut but also fortifying our defenses against everyday challenges, ensuring we stay at our best to tackle life's hurdles.

In addition to physical health benefits, the consumption of probiotics can foster a positive relationship with food. As we become more aware of the connection between our diet and mental health, embracing foods rich in probiotics can transform how we view meals. Instead of merely fueling our bodies, we start to see food as a source of joy and wellness. This shift in perspective can empower young adults and teens to make healthier choices, ultimately leading to a more balanced lifestyle that prioritizes mental and emotional well-being.

Embracing probiotics is about more than just gut health; it's a step towards a happier, healthier life. By understanding their role in our overall wellness, we can actively choose to incorporate these beneficial bacteria into our diets. Whether through delicious fermented foods or probiotic supplements, making this simple adjustment can have a profound impact on our mental health. So, let's celebrate the power of probiotics and take charge of our gut health, as it's not just about feeling good physically, but also nurturing our minds and spirits along the way!

FERMENTED FOODS FOR A HAPPIER GUT

Fermented foods are not just trendy additions to your meals; they are powerful allies in nurturing a happier gut and, ultimately, a brighter mood. Picture this: you're enjoying a tangy serving of kimchi or a creamy dollop of yogurt, and not only are your taste buds dancing, but your gut is also reaping the benefits. These foods are packed with probiotics, the beneficial bacteria that can help balance your gut microbiome. A healthy gut is linked to better digestion, improved immune function, and a positive impact on mental health. So, let's dive into the world of fermented foods and discover how they can transform your mood and overall well-being!

One of the most exciting aspects of fermented foods is their ability to enhance the gut-brain connection. Research shows that the gut microbiome communicates with the brain through various pathways, including the production of neurotransmitters. Fermented foods are rich in these probiotics, which can promote the production of serotonin, often dubbed the "happiness hormone." By incorporating foods like kefir, sauerkraut, and kombucha into your diet, you're not just supporting your digestive system; you're also giving your brain the boost it needs to help combat anxiety and depression. Imagine feeling lighter and more energized simply by indulging in delicious, tangy flavors!

Let's talk about some easy ways to add fermented foods to your daily routine. You don't need to be a culinary genius to enjoy the benefits. Start your day with a bowl of yogurt topped with fresh fruit and a sprinkle of granola. For lunch, toss some kimchi into your salad for an exciting kick. And don't forget about snacks: a refreshing kombucha or a handful of pickles can be a fun way to satisfy your cravings while supporting your mental health. These small changes can make a big difference in how you feel, both physically and emotionally.

Now, if you're wondering about the science behind it all, the evidence is compelling. Studies have shown that people who regularly consume fermented foods report lower levels of anxiety and depression. The gut microbiome is crucial in regulating stress responses, and probiotics from fermented foods can help modulate these responses. By nurturing your gut with these tasty options, you're not just feeding your body; you're also fostering a positive environment for your mental health. It's a win-win situation that's hard to resist!

As young adults and teens navigating life's challenges, it's essential to recognize the profound link between what you eat and how you feel. Fermented foods are not just a passing fad; they are a pathway to a happier, healthier you. Embracing these foods can empower you to take charge of your mental wellness while enjoying delicious flavors and textures. So go ahead, explore the world of fermentation, and let your gut lead the way to greater happiness!

HOW PROBIOTICS CAN IMPROVE MENTAL CLARITY

The connection between our gut health and mental clarity is more profound than many realize, and probiotics play a crucial role in this relationship. Imagine your gut as a bustling city, filled with diverse microorganisms working tirelessly to keep everything running smoothly. When you introduce probiotics into your diet, you're essentially sending in reinforcements to support this vibrant ecosystem. These beneficial bacteria help maintain a balanced gut microbiome, which is essential for optimal brain function. The result? Greater mental clarity and focus that can help you tackle your studies, work, or creative projects with renewed energy.

Research has shown that the gut and brain communicate through a complex network known as the gut-brain axis. This means that the health of your gut can directly impact your mental state. Probiotics can help reduce inflammation in the gut, which is often linked to mood disorders like anxiety and depression. By keeping inflammation at bay, probiotics can improve your overall mood and mental clarity, making it easier to think clearly and feel more positive. Imagine breezing through your tasks, feeling alert and present, simply by nourishing your gut with these friendly bacteria!

Incorporating probiotics into your daily routine is easier than you might think. You can find them in delicious foods like yogurt, kefir, kimchi, and sauerkraut. Each of these foods not only packs a probiotic punch but also offers a variety of flavors and textures that can spice up your meals. Whether you prefer a creamy yogurt parfait for breakfast or a zesty kimchi side dish with dinner, adding these foods to your diet can be a game changer for your mental clarity. Plus, experimenting with different probiotic-rich foods can make healthy eating an exciting adventure!

Young adults and teens can particularly benefit from probiotics, especially during times of stress like exams or major life transitions. As pressures mount, it's easy to feel overwhelmed, and that's where probiotics step in. By supporting gut health, they can help stabilize your mood and enhance your cognitive function. You may notice that when your gut feels good, so does your mind. This newfound mental clarity can aid in better decision-making, increased productivity, and a more positive outlook on life.

The journey to improved mental clarity through probiotics is not just about what you eat; it's about feeling empowered in your choices. By prioritizing gut health, you're investing in your overall well-being. So the next time you're feeling foggy or unfocused, consider what you've been eating. A small change, like adding a daily serving of probiotics, could lead to significant improvements in how you think and feel. Embrace the power of probiotics and experience the remarkable connection between your gut and your mind!

CHAPTER 6: MINDFUL EATING FOR MENTAL WELLNESS

The Practice of Mindfulness in Eating

Mindfulness in eating is a transformative practice that offers a refreshing perspective on how we approach food and its profound connection to our mental health. In a world filled with distractions, fast-paced lifestyles, and overwhelming food choices, taking a moment to truly engage with our meals can be a game changer. By focusing on the present moment, we can begin to cultivate a deeper appreciation for what we consume, leading to a more satisfying and nourishing experience. This intentional approach not only enhances our enjoyment of food but can also play a significant role in managing anxiety and depression.

Imagine sitting down for a meal without the usual interruptions of screens and notifications. By creating a calm environment, you can fully immerse yourself in the colors, textures, and aromas of your food. This practice encourages you to notice the sensations in your body as you eat, promoting a more intuitive understanding of hunger and fullness. When you listen to your body's signals, you empower yourself to make choices that align with your nutritional needs and preferences, ultimately fostering a healthier relationship with food. This awareness can help break the cycle of mindless eating, which often contributes to feelings of anxiety and dissatisfaction.

Incorporating mindfulness into your eating habits can also enhance your connection with the gut-brain axis. Research shows that what we eat directly influences our gut microbiome, which in turn affects our mood and mental clarity. By choosing whole, nutrient-rich foods and taking the time to savor each bite, you can nourish both your body and mind. Mindful eating encourages you to select foods that not only taste good but also support your overall well-being, creating a positive feedback loop that enhances your mental health. The more you fuel your body with wholesome foods, the more energized and balanced you will feel.

Moreover, practicing mindfulness in eating can serve as a powerful tool for managing stress and emotional eating. Many young adults and teens often turn to food as a way to cope with overwhelming feelings. By becoming more aware of your emotions and how they influence your eating habits, you can develop healthier coping strategies. Instead of reaching for that bag of chips when stress strikes, you might choose to pause, take a few deep breaths, and reflect on what your body truly needs in that moment. This simple shift can lead to greater self-awareness and ultimately a reduction in anxiety and depressive symptoms.

Finally, the journey of mindfulness in eating is not about strict diets or rigid rules, but rather about cultivating a joyful and compassionate relationship with food. It's about celebrating meals as opportunities to connect with yourself and others. Sharing a meal with friends or family while practicing mindfulness can deepen those connections, reinforcing the idea that food is not just fuel but also a source of joy and community. Embracing this practice can lead to a more fulfilling life, where food becomes an ally in promoting mental health and well-being. So, let's embark on this deliciously mindful adventure together, one bite at a time!

LISTENING TO YOUR BODY'S SIGNALS

Listening to your body's signals is an empowering journey that can transform your relationship with food and enhance your mental health. Every day, your body is sending you messages about what it needs, how it feels, and what might be causing it distress. This is particularly crucial for young adults and teens who are navigating the complexities of life, stress, and emotional challenges. By tuning into these signals, you can make informed choices that not only nourish your body but also support your mental well-being.

When it comes to the gut-brain connection, the signals your body sends can provide valuable insights. For instance, have you ever noticed how certain foods can leave you feeling energized while others might lead to fatigue or irritability? This is your gut communicating with your brain! Foods rich in probiotics, like yogurt or fermented vegetables, can boost your mood, while sugary snacks may lead to a quick high followed by a crash. By paying attention to these reactions, you can start to identify which foods elevate your spirits and which ones might bring you down, ultimately creating a diet that promotes a positive mindset.

Moreover, learning to listen to your body can help you recognize the early signs of anxiety or depression. You might find that certain foods exacerbate your feelings of unease or sadness. For example, a heavy, processed meal could leave you feeling sluggish, while a light, nutrient-dense meal might lift your spirits. By becoming more aware of how your food choices correlate with your emotional state, you can begin to make adjustments that foster a healthier mind. It's all about empowering yourself to take control of how you feel through the choices you make at each meal.

In addition to food choices, your body also communicates its needs through hunger and fullness cues. Many young adults and teens often struggle with diet culture pressures, leading to disconnection from these natural signals. Embracing the practice of mindfulness while eating can help you reconnect with your body. Take a moment to savor each bite, notice the flavors, and recognize when you're satisfied rather than stuffed. This not only supports a healthier relationship with food but also enhances your mental clarity and emotional stability, making it easier to navigate life's challenges.

Ultimately, listening to your body's signals is a vital step towards achieving a harmonious balance between your diet and mental health. By cultivating this awareness, you can make choices that not only satisfy your hunger but also nourish your emotional well-being. So, the next time you sit down to eat, tune in to what your body is telling you. Your gut feelings are more than just instincts; they are a roadmap to a healthier, happier you!

CREATING A POSITIVE EATING ENVIRONMENT

Creating a positive eating environment is essential for nurturing not only your physical health but also your mental well-being. Imagine a space where you feel relaxed, energized, and motivated to make healthy choices. A welcoming atmosphere can significantly enhance your relationship with food and transform your meals into joyful experiences. By focusing on the environment where you eat, you can set the stage for nourishing both your gut and your mind.

Start by considering the aesthetics of your eating area. Bright colors, natural light, and plants can uplift your mood and make your space more inviting. Ditch the clutter and create an organized area that promotes calmness. A clean dining space encourages mindfulness, allowing you to savor each bite rather than rushing through your meals. Incorporating elements like comforting textures in your table setting or listening to soothing music can further enhance your dining experience, making you feel more at ease.

It's also vital to surround yourself with positive influences during mealtimes. Eating with family and friends can lead to more enjoyable and fulfilling meals. Shared experiences, laughter, and meaningful conversations can boost your mood and reduce anxiety. If you're eating alone, consider inviting a friend over or even connecting with loved ones virtually. Socializing while dining can help you develop a healthier relationship with food and lessen feelings of isolation, which are often linked to anxiety and depression.

Mindful eating is another crucial component of a positive eating environment. Take the time to appreciate your food—its colors, textures, and flavors. By focusing on the sensory experience of eating, you can foster a deeper connection with your meals. This practice not only enhances your enjoyment but also promotes better digestion and nutrient absorption, which are vital for mental health. Set aside distractions like phones or televisions, and dedicate this time to truly savor what you're consuming.

Lastly, be intentional about the foods you bring into your environment. Stocking your kitchen with whole, nutrient-dense foods can directly impact your mood and energy levels. Fill your pantry with colorful fruits, vibrant vegetables, and wholesome grains. The act of preparing and enjoying these foods can become a joyful ritual that nurtures both your gut and your mind. As you create a positive eating environment, you'll find that it not only enhances your meals but also significantly contributes to your overall mental health and well-being.

CHAPTER 7: MEAL PLANNING FOR A HEALTHY MIND

Easy Meal Prep Ideas for Busy Lives

Meal prepping can be a game changer for busy young adults and teens looking to nourish their bodies and minds. By dedicating just a few hours each week to preparing meals, you can set yourself up for success, ensuring that healthy options are always within reach. This not only saves time but also reduces the temptation to grab unhealthy snacks or fast food when you're pressed for time. Let's explore some easy meal prep ideas that will keep your gut happy and your mental health thriving!

Start with versatile ingredients that can be transformed into various dishes. Think grains like quinoa or brown rice, which serve as a fantastic base for meals. Cook a large batch at the beginning of the week and use it as a foundation for salads, bowls, or stir-fries. Pair it with roasted vegetables, which are not only delicious but packed with nutrients that support gut health. Seasoning them with herbs and spices can elevate your meals, making each dish exciting and satisfying. The best part? You'll have meals ready to go, reducing stress during hectic days.

Don't forget about protein! Incorporating lean proteins like chicken, turkey, tofu, or legumes can help stabilize mood and energy levels. You can grill or bake a batch of chicken at the start of the week, then use it in wraps, salads, or as a topping for grain bowls. For a vegetarian option, prepare a big pot of chili or lentil stew. These hearty meals are not only comforting but also rich in fiber, which plays a crucial role in gut health and, in turn, supports mental well-being.

Snacks are often the downfall of healthy eating, but with some simple prep, they can become a highlight of your day. Create grab-and-go snack packs using fresh fruits, cut-up veggies, and wholesome dips like hummus or guacamole. You can also whip up energy bites using oats, nut butter, and seeds. These little treats are perfect for a quick boost in energy during study sessions or after school activities. By having nutritious snacks at your fingertips, you'll be less likely to reach for sugary options that might lead to energy crashes and mood swings.

Finally, don't underestimate the power of smoothies! They are quick to prepare and can be a delicious way to pack in a variety of nutrients. Pre-portion your ingredients in freezer bags, so all you need to do is blend them with your favorite liquid in the morning or after a workout. Experiment with different combinations of fruits, veggies, and even some superfoods like spinach or chia seeds. These smoothies can provide a refreshing start to your day or a revitalizing pick-me-up when you need it most. By making meal prep a part of your routine, you'll nourish your body and mind, helping you tackle life's challenges with confidence and a smile!

HOW TO CREATE A MOOD-BOOSTING GROCERY LIST

Creating a mood-boosting grocery list is an empowering way to take charge of your mental health while enjoying the process of selecting foods that can uplift your spirits. Start by thinking about the vibrant colors and textures of fresh produce that can brighten your day. Fill your cart with an array of fruits and vegetables such as sweet berries, crunchy carrots, and leafy greens. These foods are not only pleasing to the eye but also pack a powerful punch of vitamins and antioxidants that support brain function. The more colorful your cart, the more nutrients you're bringing into your life!

Next, consider incorporating whole grains into your list. Foods like quinoa, brown rice, and oats are fantastic sources of complex carbohydrates that help regulate serotonin levels in the brain. Serotonin is often dubbed the "feel-good" neurotransmitter, making it essential for maintaining a positive mood. Stocking up on these hearty grains can provide sustained energy and keep those mood swings at bay. Plus, they are incredibly versatile and can be used in numerous delicious recipes, making meal prep an exciting adventure.

Don't forget to include sources of healthy fats, which are crucial for optimal brain health. Avocados, nuts, seeds, and fatty fish like salmon are rich in omega-3 fatty acids that are known to combat anxiety and depression. They not only help improve brain function but also enhance your overall emotional well-being. Imagine whipping up a creamy avocado toast or a refreshing salmon salad; these meals can be both delicious and beneficial for your mood. By prioritizing these healthy fats, you're nurturing your brain while treating your taste buds.

In addition to whole foods, it's essential to include some feel-good snacks on your list. Dark chocolate, for example, is a delightful treat that can actually boost your mood due to its ability to increase endorphin levels. Choosing snacks with probiotics, like yogurt or kefir, can also support gut health, which is intricately linked to mental health. When you snack mindfully, you're not only satisfying your cravings but also fueling your body with nutrients that promote happiness.

Finally, remember to keep your grocery list flexible and fun. Experiment with new recipes and explore different cuisines that excite your palate. Adding a few items that spark joy, like your favorite herbal teas or fresh herbs, can make a significant difference in how you feel. The act of creating your list can be a creative outlet, inspiring you to explore the vast world of flavors while nurturing your mental health. By consciously selecting foods that uplift you, you're taking a vital step towards enhancing your mood and overall well-being.

QUICK AND NUTRITIOUS RECIPES TO TRY

Eating well doesn't have to be a chore, especially when you can whip up quick and nutritious recipes that are not only good for your body but also beneficial for your mind. Here are some delightful recipes that can support your mental health while satisfying your taste buds. Whether you're a busy student or a young professional, these meals are designed to be made in a flash, leaving you with more time to focus on what really matters—your well-being.

First up is the vibrant Buddha Bowl, a colorful mix of quinoa, roasted veggies, and a sprinkle of seeds. Start by cooking a cup of quinoa, which serves as a fantastic source of protein and fiber. While the quinoa cooks, chop up your favorite vegetables—think sweet potatoes, bell peppers, and broccoli—and toss them in olive oil and your favorite spices. Roast them in the oven for about 20 minutes. Once everything is ready, assemble your bowl by layering the quinoa, veggies, and topping it off with a handful of seeds like pumpkin or sunflower for that extra crunch. This meal not only fills you up but also fuels your brain with nutrients that promote emotional well-being.

Next, let's talk about smoothies. They're quick, versatile, and packed with nutrients. A delightful Berry Banana Smoothie can be your go-to for a refreshing breakfast or a midday snack.

Blend together a banana, a handful of mixed berries, a scoop of Greek yogurt, and a splash of almond milk. Berries are rich in antioxidants, which help combat oxidative stress, while bananas provide potassium and magnesium—minerals known to boost mood and reduce anxiety. In just five minutes, you can enjoy a delicious drink that fuels both your body and your mind.

For those times when you need a hearty meal, try a Chickpea Stir-Fry. Start by sautéing garlic and onion in a pan, then add a can of drained chickpeas, your choice of chopped vegetables, and a splash of soy sauce. Stir-fry everything for about 10 minutes until heated through. Chickpeas are an excellent source of protein and fiber, helping to keep you full and satisfied, while also contributing to a balanced gut microbiome. This dish is not only quick to prepare but also provides the nutrients your brain craves, making it an ideal option for combating feelings of anxiety or depression.

Finally, consider preparing Overnight Oats as a convenient breakfast option that you can prepare in advance. Mix rolled oats with your choice of milk, a dollop of yogurt, and your favorite toppings such as fruits, nuts, or honey. Let the mixture sit in the fridge overnight, and by morning, you'll have a delicious and nutritious meal ready to go. Oats are rich in fiber and help regulate blood sugar levels, which can positively impact your mood throughout the day. With just a little effort, you can ensure your mornings start on a positive note, setting the tone for a productive day ahead.

These quick and nutritious recipes are not just about filling your stomach; they are about nurturing your mind and soul. By incorporating these meals into your routine, you can actively support your mental health and enhance your overall well-being. So grab your ingredients and get cooking—your gut and your mind will thank you!

CHAPTER 8: OVERCOMING FOOD MYTHS

Debunking Common Diet Misconceptions

Diet misconceptions can often cloud our understanding of how food influences our mental health, particularly for young adults and teens navigating the complexities of life. One common myth is that all fats are bad for you. The truth is, healthy fats, such as those found in avocados, nuts, and olive oil, are essential for brain health. They help maintain the structure of brain cells and support cognitive function. Embracing these nutritious fats can actually enhance mood and reduce anxiety, proving that not all fats are the enemy!

Another prevalent myth is that carbs should be completely avoided for optimal health. While it's true that refined carbs can lead to energy crashes and mood swings, complex carbohydrates found in whole grains, fruits, and vegetables are vital for mental well-being. They release glucose slowly into the bloodstream, providing a steady source of energy for the brain. This steady supply can help stabilize mood and prevent those dreaded afternoon slumps when anxiety and irritability can spike. So, don't shy away from carbs; instead, choose the right kinds to fuel your brain!

Many believe that skipping meals is an effective way to lose weight and improve health. However, this misconception can have detrimental effects on mental health. Skipping meals can lead to low blood sugar, which often results in irritability, fatigue, and even anxiety. Regular, balanced meals provide the nutrients your brain needs to function optimally and keep your mood stable. Instead of skipping meals, focusing on nourishing your body with a variety of foods will support both your physical and mental health.

Another myth that deserves debunking is the idea that supplements can replace a healthy diet. While certain vitamins and minerals are crucial for mental health, they should complement a nutritious diet rather than serve as a replacement. Whole foods are packed with a complex array of nutrients that work synergistically to support mood and cognitive function. Relying solely on supplements might leave you lacking essential components necessary for overall well-being. It's all about balance and ensuring that your plate is colorful and diverse!

Finally, let's tackle the notion that food and mental health are separate entities. This misconception can lead to neglecting the profound impact that diet has on emotional well-being. Research shows that what you eat can significantly influence your mood, stress levels, and overall mental health. By understanding and embracing the gut-brain connection, you can make informed dietary choices that boost your mental resilience. Eating mindfully and choosing nutrient-rich foods can empower you to take charge of your mental health, creating a positive cycle of well-being that benefits both body and mind!

THE TRUTH ABOUT FAD DIETS AND MENTAL HEALTH

Fad diets are everywhere, promising rapid weight loss and a quick fix to your body image issues. But beneath the surface allure of these trendy eating patterns lies a complex relationship with mental health that often goes unaddressed. For young adults, teens, and women, the pressure to conform to social media ideals can lead to a whirlwind of emotions. The truth is that while these diets may offer temporary results, they can wreak havoc on your mental well-being, exacerbating feelings of anxiety and depression rather than alleviating them.

The gut-brain connection is a fascinating area of research that reveals how our diet influences our mood and mental health. When embarking on a restrictive fad diet, you might think you're doing something positive for your body. However, these diets can limit essential nutrients that support brain function. A lack of vital vitamins and minerals can lead to increased irritability and mood swings, making it harder to cope with daily stressors. It's crucial to recognize that what you eat doesn't just affect your physical health; it also plays a significant role in how you feel emotionally.

Many fad diets promote an all-or-nothing mindset, creating an unhealthy relationship with food. This can lead to feelings of guilt and shame when you indulge in a "forbidden" food or stray from the rigid rules. For young women and teens who are often navigating identity and self-worth, this can be particularly damaging. Instead of fostering a balanced approach to eating, these diets can fuel disordered eating patterns, causing a vicious cycle of restriction and bingeing that negatively impacts mental health.

Moreover, the social aspect of eating is often overlooked in fad diet culture. Sharing meals with friends and family is a vital part of human connection, yet these diets can isolate individuals, making them feel like they can't enjoy food in a social setting. This loneliness can intensify feelings of anxiety and depression, leading to a disconnect not only from food but also from loved ones. Understanding the importance of community and shared experiences can empower young adults and teens to break free from the constraints of fad diets and embrace a more holistic approach to nutrition.

Ultimately, the truth about fad diets is that they often do more harm than good, especially when it comes to mental health. Instead of chasing quick fixes, it's essential to focus on building a sustainable, balanced diet that nourishes both your body and mind. Prioritizing whole foods rich in nutrients, engaging in mindful eating practices, and fostering a positive relationship with food can lead to improved mental health outcomes. By taking charge of your diet in a way that uplifts rather than restricts, you can cultivate a happier, healthier mindset that supports your overall well-being.

EMBRACING A SUSTAINABLE EATING HABIT

Embracing a sustainable eating habit is not just a trend; it's a powerful choice that can transform your mental health and overall well-being. As young adults and teens, you have the unique opportunity to shape your dietary habits, not only for your own benefit but also for the planet's. Imagine indulging in delicious meals that not only nourish your body but also create a positive ripple effect on the environment. By choosing sustainable foods, you're making a conscious decision to support eco-friendly practices while also enhancing your gut health, which is intricately linked to your emotional well-being.

Sustainable eating often means opting for whole, plant-based foods that are rich in nutrients and low in harmful additives. Fresh fruits, vegetables, whole grains, and legumes are not only fantastic for your gut microbiome but also help to stabilize your mood. When you consume a diet packed with these foods, you're providing your body with the essential vitamins and minerals it needs to thrive. This, in turn, can lead to a reduction in anxiety and depressive symptoms, giving you the fuel to navigate the ups and downs of young adulthood with confidence and clarity.

Moreover, sustainable eating encourages mindfulness and intentionality around food choices. When you become aware of where your food comes from and the impact it has on the environment, you develop a deeper appreciation for the meals you consume. This mindfulness can translate into better decision-making when it comes to your diet. Preparing meals with intention allows you to connect with your food on a personal level, fostering a sense of gratitude that can uplift your spirit and enhance your mental health.

Incorporating local and seasonal ingredients into your meals is another exciting way to embrace sustainability. Not only does it support local farmers and reduce your carbon footprint, but it also means that you're likely consuming fresher produce that is packed with flavor and nutrients. Think about how invigorating it feels to bite into a juicy, ripe tomato or a crisp apple. These experiences not only satisfy your taste buds but also nourish your gut, which, as research shows, plays a crucial role in regulating your mood.

Finally, remember that embracing sustainable eating isn't about perfection; it's about progress. Start small by making one sustainable change at a time, whether it's swapping out processed snacks for homemade granola bars or exploring plant-based meal options. Celebrate each step you take toward a healthier you and a healthier planet. As you cultivate these habits, you'll likely notice a shift not only in your physical health but also in your mental clarity and emotional resilience. So, gather your friends, get creative in the kitchen, and embark on this delicious journey toward sustainable eating for a happier, healthier life!

CHAPTER 9: THE ROLE OF LIFESTYLE IN MENTAL HEALTH

Exercise: The Perfect Partner to Nutrition

Exercise is not just a physical activity; it's a powerful ally in the quest for mental well-being. For young adults, teens, and women navigating the complexities of life, incorporating regular exercise can be a game-changer. When paired with a balanced diet, exercise amplifies the benefits of nutrition, creating a synergistic effect that enhances mood and mental clarity. Imagine combining healthy meals that nourish your gut with the invigorating rush of a workout, resulting in a more upbeat, energetic, and positive outlook on life.

As we delve deeper into the gut-brain connection, it becomes clear that movement plays a pivotal role in this relationship. Exercise stimulates the production of neurotransmitters like serotonin and dopamine, which are crucial for regulating mood and reducing feelings of anxiety and depression. When you break a sweat, your body releases endorphins, often referred to as "feel-good" hormones. This natural high not only improves your mood but also helps in managing stress levels. For young adults and teens facing academic pressures or social challenges, this boost can make a significant difference.

Moreover, engaging in physical activities can improve gut health, which in turn supports mental well-being. Regular exercise promotes healthy digestion, enhancing the gut microbiome, which is closely linked to mental health. A balanced gut microbiome can lead to better nutrient absorption, ensuring your brain receives the essential vitamins and minerals it needs to function optimally. Women, in particular, may find that maintaining an active lifestyle can alleviate symptoms related to hormonal fluctuations, further stabilizing mood and emotional health.

Finding the right type of exercise can be the key to sustaining motivation and enjoyment. Whether it's dancing, yoga, running, or team sports, the options are endless! The most important thing is to choose activities that resonate with you and fit seamlessly into your lifestyle. This personal connection to exercise not only makes it more enjoyable but also increases the likelihood of sticking with it. Pairing your favorite workouts with nutritious meals creates a holistic approach to health that supports both body and mind.

Incorporating exercise into your daily routine can be an exciting journey towards a healthier you. It's about finding balance and recognizing that nutrition and physical activity go hand in hand in shaping your mental health. Embrace this dynamic duo and witness the transformation in your energy levels, mood stability, and overall mental clarity. As you nourish your body with wholesome foods and invigorate it with movement, you'll discover that the path to mental wellness is not just achievable but incredibly fulfilling.

SLEEP: RESTING FOR A SHARPER MIND

Sleep is not just a luxury; it's a necessity for a sharper mind and a healthier gut. For young adults, teens, and women navigating the whirlwind of life, prioritizing sleep can make a world of difference in how you feel both mentally and physically. Imagine waking up refreshed, ready to tackle challenges, and equipped to handle whatever comes your way. Quality sleep enhances cognitive function, improves mood, and sharpens your focus, making it an essential component of your overall well-being.

The connection between sleep and mental health is undeniable. When you're well-rested, your brain is more adept at managing stress, anxiety, and even symptoms of depression. Lack of sleep can create a vicious cycle, where increased anxiety leads to sleepless nights, and those sleepless nights amplify anxiety. By prioritizing sleep, you can break this cycle and foster a more resilient mindset. It's about creating a nurturing environment for your brain, allowing it to recharge and reset, paving the way for a clearer, more positive outlook.

One of the most fascinating aspects of sleep is its relationship with your gut health. The gut-brain connection plays a pivotal role in how you feel, and sleep is a vital part of that equation. When you sleep well, your gut bacteria flourish, promoting the production of neurotransmitters like serotonin, which is crucial for mood regulation. Conversely, poor sleep can disrupt this delicate balance, leading to digestive issues and mood swings. By ensuring you get enough quality sleep, you not only support your mental health but also create a thriving environment for your gut.

To enhance your sleep quality, consider the impact of your diet. Foods rich in omega-3 fatty acids, antioxidants, and vitamins can help regulate sleep patterns. Think about incorporating whole grains, leafy greens, and healthy fats into your evening meals. Additionally, be mindful of caffeine and sugar intake, especially in the hours leading up to bedtime. Creating a calming bedtime routine, perhaps paired with a soothing herbal tea, can signal to your body that it's time to wind down, further supporting your journey to restful nights and sharper days.

Finally, let's acknowledge that sleep is not a one-size-fits-all solution. Everyone's needs are different, and it's important to listen to your body. Experiment with your sleep schedule, create a cozy sleep sanctuary, and prioritize relaxation techniques like meditation or deep breathing. By investing in your sleep, you're investing in your mental health, harnessing the power of rest to unlock your full potential. Embrace the magic of sleep—your mind, body, and gut will thank you!

STRESS MANAGEMENT TECHNIQUES

Stress is an inevitable part of life, especially for young adults and teens navigating the challenges of school, relationships, and future career paths. However, managing that stress effectively can make a significant difference in your overall mental health. One of the most exciting aspects of stress management is the strong connection between what we eat and how we feel. By incorporating certain stress-busting foods and techniques into your daily routine, you can harness the power of your diet to create a more balanced and positive mindset.

One effective technique for managing stress is incorporating omega-3 fatty acids into your meals. These essential fats, found in fatty fish like salmon, walnuts, and flaxseeds, have been shown to support brain health and reduce anxiety. By making omega-3s a staple in your diet, you not only nourish your body but also provide your brain with the tools it needs to combat stress. Imagine enjoying a delicious salmon salad or a smoothie packed with flaxseeds while knowing that you're fueling your body and mind to handle whatever life throws your way!

Another powerful stress management strategy is practicing mindfulness while you eat. This technique involves slowing down and savoring each bite, paying attention to the flavors and textures of your food. Not only does this practice enhance your enjoyment of meals, but it also allows you to tune into your body's signals, helping you recognize how certain foods affect your mood and stress levels. Create a calming atmosphere at mealtime, free from distractions, and embrace each moment. This simple shift can transform your relationship with food, making it a source of nourishment and comfort rather than just a means to an end.

Physical activity is another dynamic way to manage stress, and it can be even more effective when paired with a nutritious diet. Engaging in regular exercise releases endorphins, the body's natural mood lifters, which can significantly reduce feelings of anxiety and stress. Consider activities that you genuinely enjoy, whether it's dancing, yoga, or a brisk walk in nature. Combine this with a balanced diet rich in fruits, vegetables, and whole grains, and you'll create a powerhouse of positivity that fuels both your body and mind.

Finally, don't underestimate the impact of community and social support on stress management. Sharing meals with friends or family not only enhances the enjoyment of food but also fosters connections that can help you cope with life's ups and downs. Organize a potluck dinner or a cooking night with friends where everyone contributes a healthy dish. These moments of togetherness not only nourish your body but also strengthen your emotional resilience. Embrace the power of food and connection, and watch how your stress levels begin to diminish, paving the way for a healthier, happier you.

CHAPTER 10: YOUR JOURNEY TO A HEALTHIER MIND AND GUT

Creating Your Personal Action Plan

Creating your personal action plan is an exciting opportunity to take charge of your mental health and well-being through the food choices you make every day. This plan is not just a set of goals; it's a powerful commitment to nurturing your mind and body by understanding the crucial gut-brain connection. As young adults and teens, you hold the key to transforming your relationship with food, and this journey begins with a thoughtful, personalized approach tailored to your unique lifestyle and preferences.

Start by assessing your current eating habits. Reflect on what you eat regularly, how you feel after meals, and any emotional connections you have with certain foods. Take some time to journal about your experiences with food and mood. Are there specific foods that uplift your spirits or others that seem to drag you down? By identifying patterns in your eating behavior, you can begin to pinpoint areas for improvement. This self-awareness is the first step in crafting a plan that aligns more closely with your mental health goals.

Next, set clear, achievable goals that resonate with you. Instead of overwhelming yourself with a long list of changes, focus on a few key areas that you can realistically tackle. Perhaps you want to incorporate more fruits and vegetables into your meals or experiment with new recipes that include gut-friendly ingredients like fermented foods. Break these goals down into actionable steps—like trying a new recipe each week or swapping out sugary snacks for healthier alternatives. Celebrate your progress, no matter how small, as each change paves the way for better mental clarity and emotional resilience.

Don't forget to build a support system around your action plan! Share your goals with friends, family, or even social media communities that are passionate about food and mental health. Engaging with others who share your journey can provide motivation, accountability, and even inspiration for new ideas. You might discover a friend who wants to join you in meal prepping or someone who can recommend a fantastic cookbook focused on gut health. Together, you can explore the impact of diet on anxiety and depression, turning your personal action plan into a communal celebration of well-being.

Finally, make sure to regularly review and adjust your action plan as needed. Your needs may change over time, and that's perfectly okay! Keep track of how your dietary choices are affecting your mood and mental health. Are you feeling more energetic? Less anxious? More focused? Use these reflections to adapt your plan and keep it dynamic. By staying flexible and open to change, you'll not only strengthen the gut-brain connection but also cultivate a lifelong habit of prioritizing your mental health through mindful eating. Embrace this journey wholeheartedly, knowing that every positive choice you make is a step toward a brighter, healthier future!

BUILDING A SUPPORT SYSTEM

Building a support system is crucial for anyone navigating the complex relationship between diet and mental health, especially for young adults and teens. The journey towards understanding how what we eat influences our emotional well-being can feel overwhelming, but having a solid support system in place can make all the difference. Friends, family, and even online communities can provide encouragement, share experiences, and offer insights that can lighten the load. Surrounding yourself with individuals who understand the gut-brain connection can empower you to make healthier choices and inspire you to stay committed to your mental health journey.

Engaging with friends who share similar interests in food and nutrition can create a vibrant atmosphere for discussing mental health. Organizing cooking nights or meal prep sessions can turn healthy eating into a fun, social activity. Imagine chopping vegetables with your best friends while chatting about the latest research on how probiotics can boost mood and reduce anxiety. This shared experience not only strengthens bonds but also reinforces the importance of healthy eating as a collective effort. When you have a tribe that values mental health and nutrition, you're more likely to stay motivated and inspired to make positive changes.

Don't underestimate the power of social media and online communities. Platforms like Instagram and TikTok are filled with content creators who focus on the gut-brain connection and share their journeys with food and mental health. By following these influencers, you can find recipes, tips, and a sense of belonging. Joining online forums or support groups dedicated to mental health and nutrition can also provide a safe space for you to express your struggles and triumphs. These communities can offer advice, share experiences, and remind you that you're not alone on this journey.

Family can also play a pivotal role in your support system. Opening up to your family about your mental health challenges and the dietary changes you want to make can foster understanding and support. They can help by participating in family meals that prioritize nutrition or encouraging healthier choices at home. When families work together to create an environment that promotes mental well-being through diet, it becomes easier for everyone to thrive. Plus, sharing educational resources about the impact of diet on mental health can empower your loved ones to join you in this transformative journey.

Finally, consider seeking professional guidance to round out your support system. Therapists, nutritionists, and dietitians can provide valuable insights tailored specifically to your needs. Many professionals understand the intricate relationship between diet and mental health, and they can equip you with strategies to improve your gut health and, consequently, your mood. Having experts on your side can enhance your understanding of how food choices affect your mental state, providing you with the tools to build a healthier, happier you. With a strong support system in place, you'll be well on your way to embracing a lifestyle that nurtures both your gut and your mind.

CELEBRATING SMALL WINS ON YOUR PATH TO WELLNESS

Celebrating small wins on your path to wellness is not just a motivational phrase; it's a powerful practice that can transform your mental health journey. As young adults and teens navigating the complexities of life, recognizing and celebrating these small victories can provide a significant boost to your overall well-being. Whether it's choosing a healthy snack over junk food, cooking a nutritious meal for yourself, or simply taking a moment to appreciate how certain foods make you feel, each of these accomplishments deserves recognition. By acknowledging your progress, no matter how minor it may seem, you create a positive feedback loop that encourages further healthy choices.

Imagine waking up one morning and deciding to swap out your usual sugary breakfast for a bowl of oatmeal topped with fresh fruits and nuts. That might seem like a small change, but it's a step toward better gut health and improved mood! When you celebrate such choices, you reinforce the connection between your diet and mental wellness. Each time you make a healthier decision, you're not just feeding your body; you're nourishing your mind. This simple act of acknowledgment can empower you to continue making choices that support your gut-brain connection, ultimately leading to a more vibrant, balanced life.

Another exciting way to celebrate small wins is by tracking your progress. Keeping a journal or using an app to log your meals and how they make you feel can illuminate patterns in your eating habits and mental state. Recognizing that a specific food boosts your mood or that a week of mindful eating leads to less anxiety can be incredibly motivating. When you look back and see how far you've come, it's a reminder of your strength and resilience. Each entry becomes a testament to your commitment to wellness, helping you to stay focused on your goals while enjoying the journey.

Social support plays a crucial role in celebrating your wins, too! Share your accomplishments with friends, family, or an online community. Whether it's posting about your healthy meal prep or talking about how you felt after a week of mindful eating, celebrating together amplifies the joy. It creates a sense of camaraderie and accountability, reminding you that you're not alone in your pursuit of wellness. Plus, you might inspire others to embark on their own health journeys, creating a ripple effect of positivity and motivation.

Lastly, remember that the journey to wellness is not always linear, and that's perfectly okay. Some days will be tougher than others, but recognizing the small wins—even on challenging days—can help you maintain a positive outlook. Whether it's simply getting through a stressful day or choosing to drink more water, each step counts. Embrace the idea that every effort you make is a building block toward a healthier mind and body. So, celebrate those small wins! They are the stepping stones that lead to greater achievements on your path to a fulfilling and balanced life.